THE KEMNAY ST

JAMES WINNETT

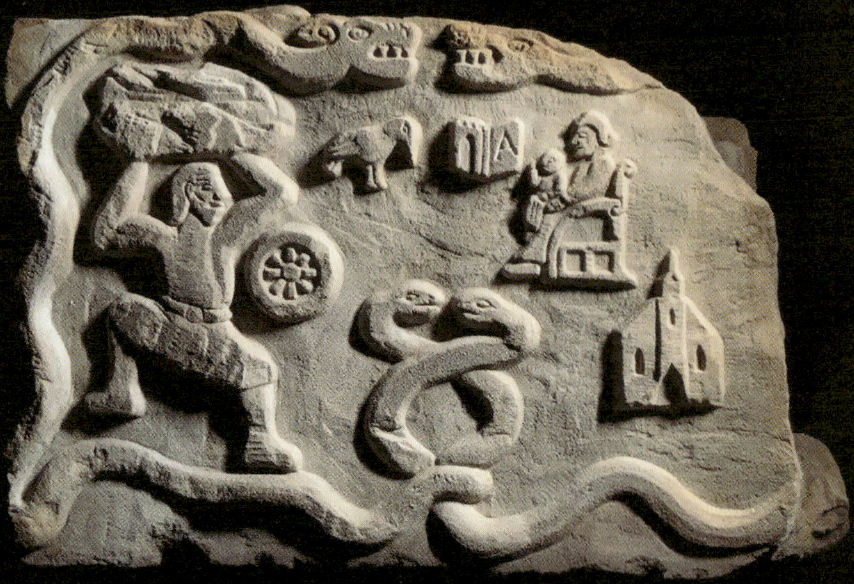

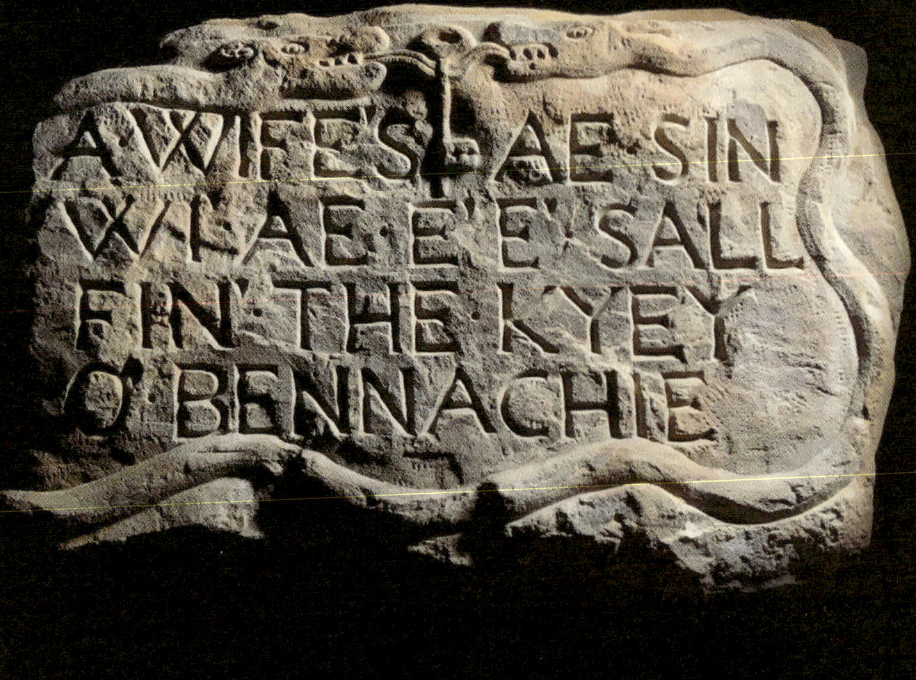
A WIFES LAE ES IN
WI AE E E' SALL
FIN' THE KYEY
O' BENNACHIE

The Jock o' Bennachie Steen

This rectangular stone is carved on four sides and can be found off Greystone Road, an area of high ground above Bogbeth. It is said that the giant Jock o' Bennachie once guarded the hills on the horizon north of Kemnay. He slept at Little John's Length and dried his clothes on a slope north-west of Craigshannoch. From Bennachie he hurled boulders at his numerous foes on the hills of Barra, Dunydeer and Noth.

The stone's south face shows Jock with a great boulder poised above his head. Jock's greatest rival was his neighbour Jock o' Noth, who lived on Tap o' Noth above Rhynie to the north-west. Tap o' Noth was once the site of a major Pictish hillfort with recent research suggesting the surrounding settlement may once have been the largest in early medieval Britain. Mither Tap on Bennachie was also the site of a substantial Pictish era hillfort.

Two dog-like beasts can be seen in confrontation towards the top of the carving, their serpentine forms framing the stone. Below, their bodies entwine as snakes taking the form of a caduceus - a symbol associated with the Greek messenger to the gods Hermes and his Roman equivalent Mercury. The caduceus was said to be able to wake the sleeping and send the awake to sleep.

The seated figure to the right represents St Anne, mother of Mary, to whom the early kirk in Kemnay was dedicated. Jock was also said to have thrown a huge granite boulder at the kirk but it overshot and landed in a field above Bogbeth. Now known as the Greystone this gigantic erratic can be seen nearby.

Jock's final bout was against his great rival Jock o' Noth, although this time they were competing for the affection of Lady Anne, a giant who lived locally. Jock, seeing them together on Tap o' Noth, was so unhappy that he hurled another great boulder in their direction. At that moment, Jock o' Noth raised up a stone of his own and in doing so put Lady Anne in the path of the other flying rock, which seemingly killed her where she stood. Seeing what he had done, Jock o' Bennachie was horrified. However, he was later visited on Bennachie by a strange woman. Convinced that this was Lady Anne, it is said that when they kissed a sudden darkness came all around and he fell into an enchanted sleep beneath his mountain home.

The east face of the stone shows a sleeping Jock entombed beneath Bennachie, surrounded by a serpent eating its own a tail. Known as an ouroboros, this ancient symbol has multiple interpretations often linked to the cycle of life and death and the cyclical nature of the year.

Above the mountain, a raven and a triple-faced carving suggest an association with Lugh, a Celtic warrior deity whose feast day falls on 1st August. Known as Lùnastal in Scotland or Lammas, it is one of the four Celtic seasonal festivals along with Samhain, Imbolc and

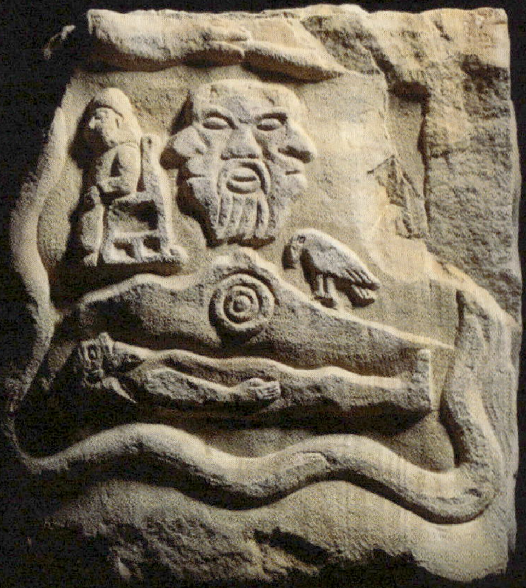

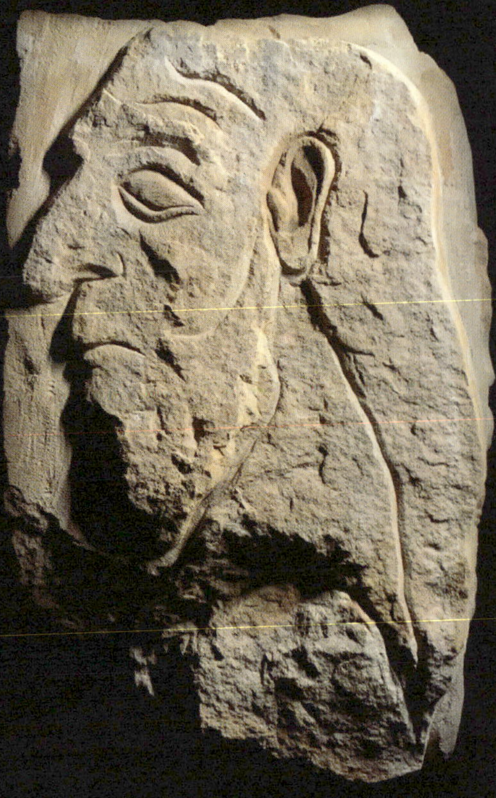

Beltane. Lùnastal was a time of hilltop gatherings, trading and athletic contests. It heralded the beginning of the harvest, a time of great celebration when cattle were brought down from their summer pastures.

The sleeping face of Jock o' Bennachie can be seen on the upper surface of the stone. It bears some resemblance to the 6th century carving of the Rhynie Man.

The north face of the stone carries part of a prophecy attributed to the 13th century seer Thomas the Rhymer. The text foretells that Jock will one day be freed when the key to the mountain is found by an only son with one eye:

A WIFE'S AE SIN WI' AE E'E
SALL FIN' THE KYEY O' BENNACHIE

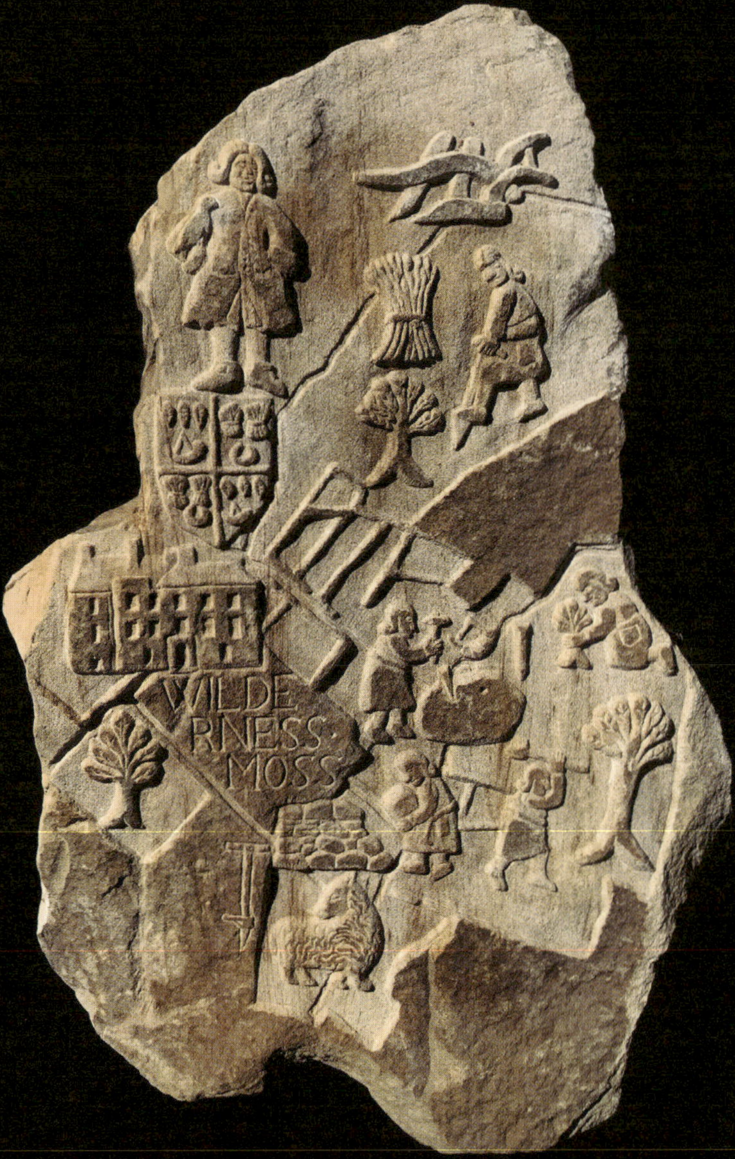

WILDE
RNESS
MOSS

The Improving Laird Steen

This wedge-shaped stone can be found on the south-west edge of Bogbeth Park, an area described as 'very wet and mossy' on a map from 1790.[1] The stone references the improvements to the local agricultural landscape that took place in the 18th century, particularly under the watch of George Burnett of Kemnay (1714-1780).

George was the first of the 'Improving Lairds' of Kemnay. Here he is shown standing above his coat of arms, overseeing the work taking place on his land. A parrot can just about be seen perched on his arm. The only known painting of George, from 1721, shows him as a confident looking seven-year-old holding a multicoloured parrot.

Below George you can see fields where dykes are being constructed from cleared stones. The largest fieldstones are being blasted with explosives. There are people cutting peat and planting tree saplings, while elsewhere mature trees are harvested for their timber. The 18th century saw huge changes as the land became more productive and yields improved. New ideas came to Kemnay around crop rotation, using horses instead of oxen and growing turnips.

Kemnay House, the Burnett family home, is shown on the stone alongside the 'Wilderness' and 'Moss' to the south. An arrow on the side of the stone points the way to 'Paradyce' – the name of a wooded hill to the north, but perhaps also a reference to the improving landscape. Paradise Hill would later become the site of Kemnay Quarry.

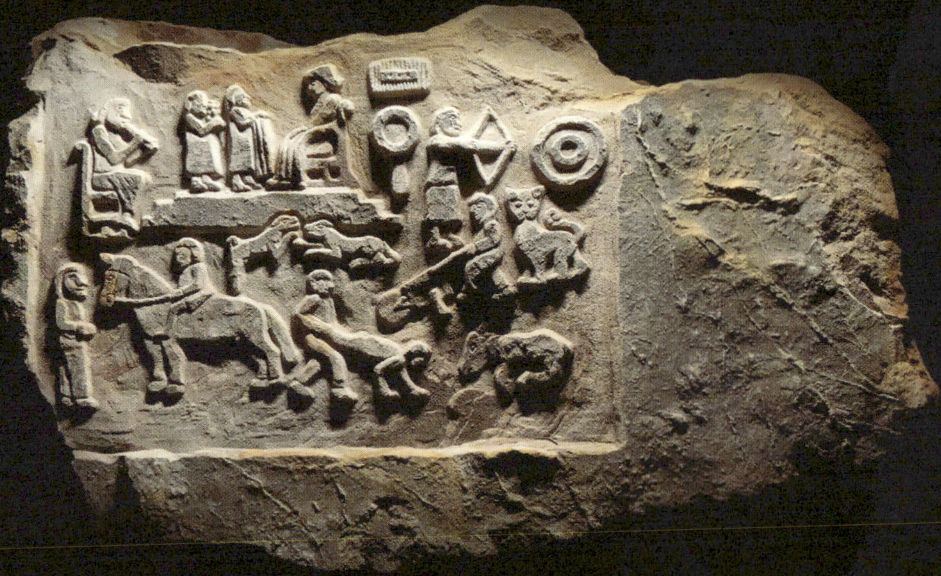

The Kemnay Fair Steen

This rectangular stone is located along a footpath on the western edge of Bogbeth Park. Carved in a style reminiscent of a Pictish stone, it tells the story of the Kemnay Fair which used to take place in the park each summer.

The Kemnay Queen can be seen in the centre of the stone on a raised platform, her attendants offering flowers and a cloak while a musician plays behind. Two dogs play fight below as an archer takes aim at a target and a child rides a horse. Participants compete in a human wheelbarrow race before the arrival of the 'Red Barrows' display team. A cat and a goat can also be seen.

All of the characters carved on the stone feature in a 1976 documentary film by G M M Thomson which captures the sights and sounds of the fair. To watch the film search online for 'Kemnay Fair 1976'.[2]

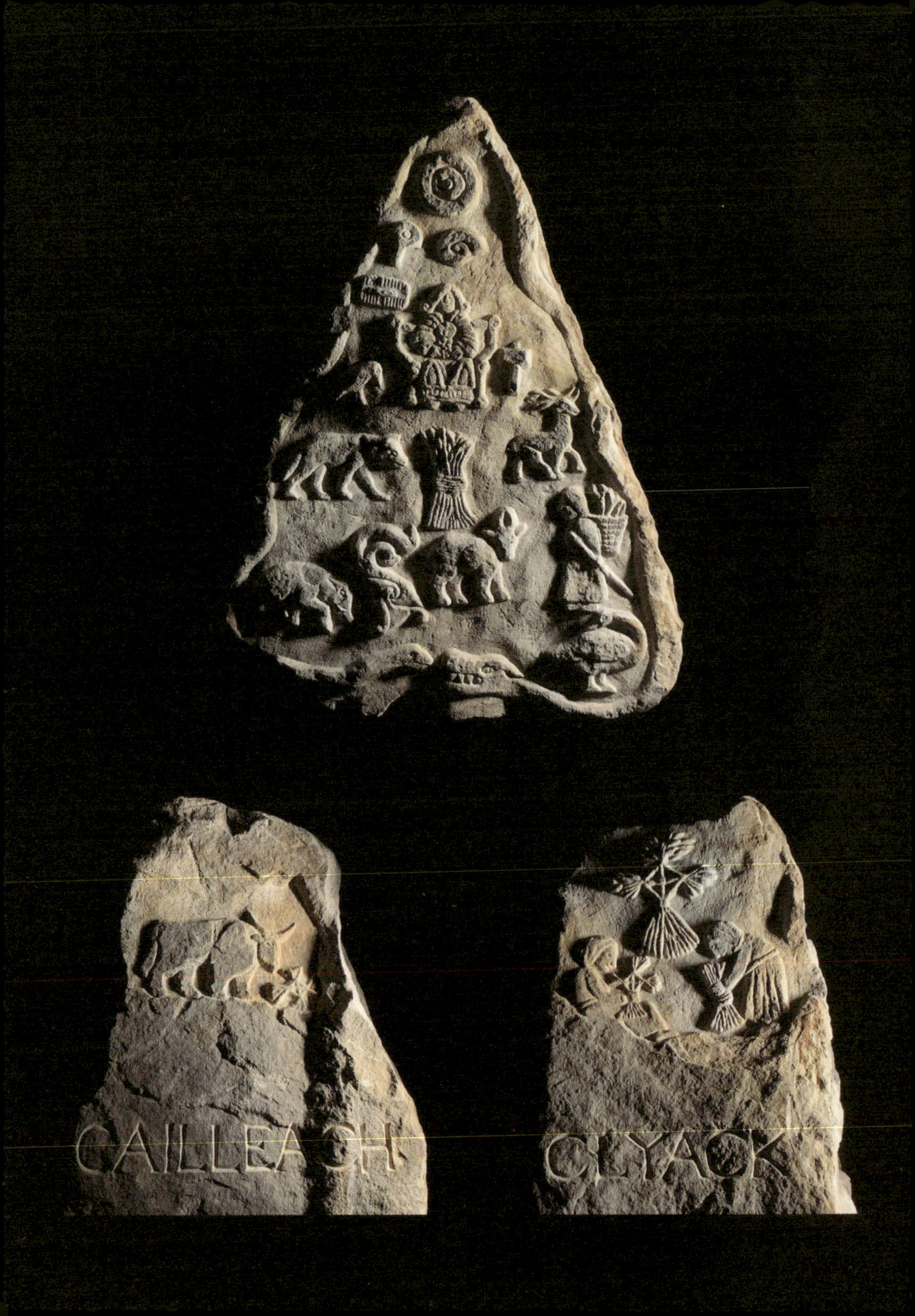
CAILLEACH
CLYACK

The Birley Bush Steen

This triangular shaped stone is situated within Birley Bush Community Garden on Grove Road. It features a number of carvings linked to old agricultural traditions, the cycle of the seasons and the relationship between the 'Clyack' and the 'Cailleach'.

The end of the harvest has long been a cause for celebration with many traditions dating back hundreds or even thousands of years. The west face of the stone shows the Clyack sheaf, the last sheaf to be cut during the harvest. The word comes from 'caileag' or girl in Gaelic. It would usually be cut with a scythe by the youngest boy present before the youngest girl gathered and bound it into the shape of a figure. Sometimes it would be dressed in women's clothes and then carried in triumph to the farmhouse where it was given pride of place in the evening's celebrations. The Clyack sheaf might be danced with to kick off the festivities before being hung up on the wall for the winter. As shown on the east face of the stone, it was then either fed to the oldest farm animal at Christmas or ploughed back into the land in the spring thus continuing the cycle.

The 'Cailleach' (literally 'old woman'), is a very old concept of the creator deity or Earth Mother in Scotland. She is associated with the wild forces of the weather and the land. On the south face of the stone she can be seen seated, flanked by a deer and a wolf over whom she is patron. At her side is the giant hammer with which she shaped the mountains and lochs. As Beira, Queen of Winter, she rules from Samhain to Beltane (November to May). With the coming of summer she transforms into the youthful Bride (or Brigid), goddess of fertility and healing who rules over the summer months.

On the right of the stone, the Cailleach can be seen collecting firewood at Imbolc, the first day of spring on 1st February (also St Bride's Day). Flocks of geese gather in the fields. Traditionally, if the weather on this day was sunny then this was a sign that the winter would go on a while longer, as she had given herself good conditions to collect wood.

Not far from the stone, at Craigearn, is an old chapel that was dedicated to St Bride before it was united with the kirk in Kemnay around 1500. Bride herself is associated with fire, wild boar and the coming of spring. She rules from Beltane on 1st May, when bonfires are lit and cattle are driven out to pasture. A symbol representing fire or a flower can be seen towards the base of the stone as spring wins out over winter and Bride, in the form of her patron animal the snake, battles with the wolf.

Lùnastal comes on 1st August with the beginning of the harvest, before Samhain arrives on 31st October, marking the end of the year, the beginning of winter and the return of the Cailleach. As mother goddess the Cailleach was linked to sovereignty; before anyone could rule the land, they first had to gain her approval. The stone itself is orientated directly with Mither Tap.

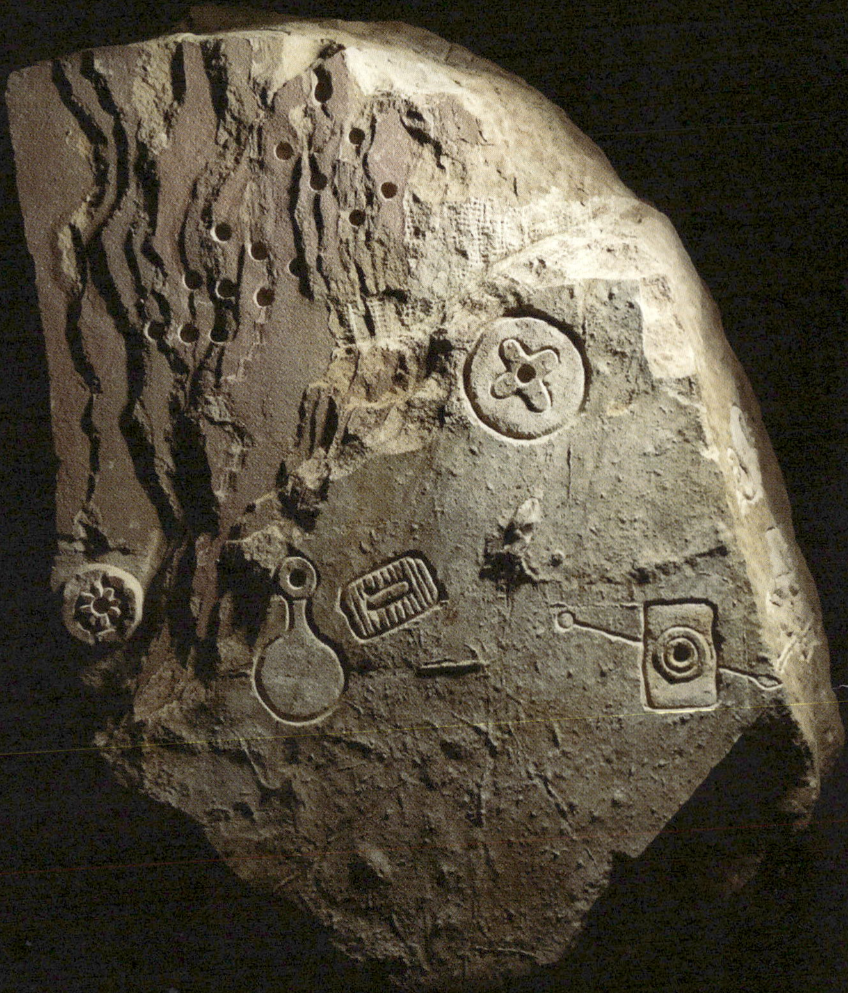

The Mither Tap Steen

Positioned on the south bank of the river Don, this stone lies downstream from the Boat of Kemnay, one of the main points for crossing the river prior to the construction of a bridge in the 1860s.

This large stone is carved with a variety of imagery and symbols, some of which connect to motifs found on the other stones. A rudimentary step has been cut into the stone, inviting the passer-by to climb up and admire the view.

The Don at this point makes a dramatic 90 degree shift in direction, sweeping to the left and flowing directly towards Bennachie. Mither Tap is particularly prominent from this viewpoint, the exposed granite of the peak and the remains of the surrounding Pictish hill fort clearly visible.

Bennachie is known as 'Beinn na Ciche' or 'hill of the breast' in Gaelic, owing to the distinctive shape of Mither Tap. The peak is visible across much of Aberdeenshire and it is likely that it had an early religious significance, with numerous standing stones and stone circles in the surrounding landscape. It has also been suggested that the name comes from 'Benne Cé', 'mountain of the people of Cé', with Cé being a Pictish territory covering the surrounding area. The hill fort itself was active during the 7th and 8th centuries.

A wheel motif can be seen on the upper face of the stone alongside a mirror and comb – a pairing frequently seen in Pictish carvings. Some of the symbols have a central circular depression as if small pebbles could be placed in them. A series of similar shallow holes appear in an arrangement similar to a lunar calendar.

Towards the edge is a rectangular shield crossed with a spear, symbols both of aggression and defence. The combination of the two is sometimes associated with Cocidius, a deity worshipped in northern Britain who the Romans equated both with Mars, god of war and Silvanus, god of forests and wild places.

The spear is aligned both with the peak of Mither Tap and with the setting sun at the summer solstice. It is similar in form to the weapons found on Pictish spearman carvings such as one from Rhynie, a major Pictish power centre of the 4th to 6th centuries.

On the side of the stone is a carving of a seated warrior accompanied by the same shield and spear. A child can be seen at her breast.

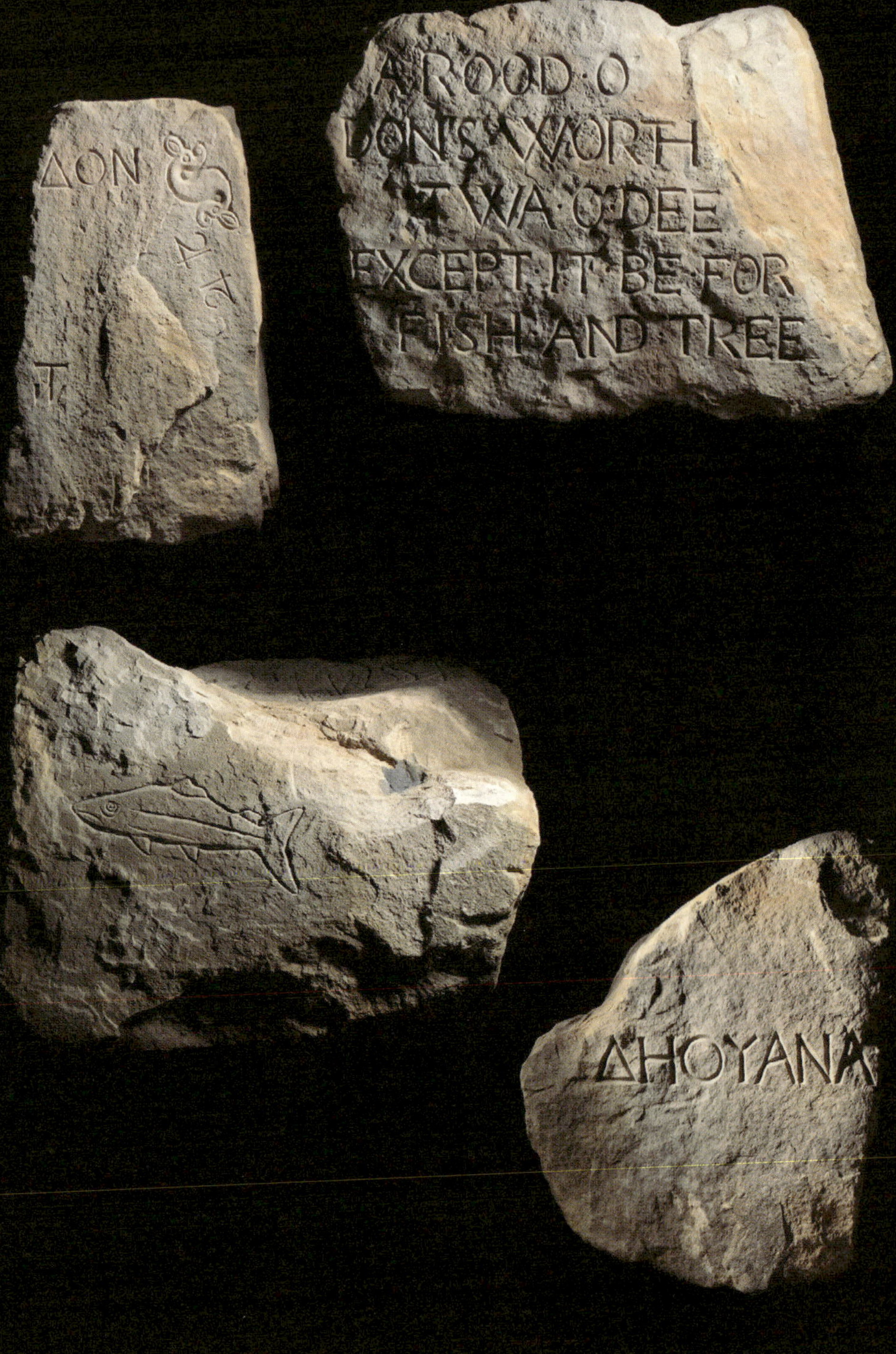
ΔΟΝ
A ROOD O
DON'S WORTH
TWA O' DEE
EXCEPT IT BE FOR
FISH AND TREE
ΔΗΟΥΑΝΑ

The River Don Steen

This stone can be found on the south bank of the Don, along a footpath that runs between Kembhill Park and the river. It carries a rich range of carvings, including the text of an old couplet comparing the merits of the Don and the Dee:

A ROOD OF DON'S WORTH TWA O' DEE,
EXCEPT IT BE FOR FISH AND TREE

The Don was said be more valuable and fertile than the Dee with a 'rood' being an old unit of measurement equal to 222 inches.

On the west face of the stone the Greek word 'ΔHOYANA' (Devona) appears. The first potential historical reference to the river was in the second century AD when the geographer Ptolemy of Alexandria in Egypt used the term which can be translated as 'deity' or 'flow'.

The east face of the stone is carved with the word 'ΔON' alongside a carving reminiscent of a Romano-British dragonesque brooch. In Welsh mythology the name 'Dôn' refers to an ancient mother goddess, with old Welsh thought to be close linguistically to the Pictish language. In this context Dôn may be associated with the Celtic mother goddess Ana, also known as Danu, meaning 'to flow'. Early Christians transformed the goddess Ana into Saint Anne, the mother of Mary.

The top of the stone has a carving of a Pictish beast, a symbol of unknown meaning which occurs frequently on Pictish stones. Suggestions for what it might represent include a dolphin, an elephant, a dragonesque brooch or the 'each uisge' water spirit. Elephants were once washed in the Don when Bostock and Wombwell's circus came to Kemnay in the early part of the 20th century.

A carving of a cow may reference the source of the Don at Brown Cow Hill or perhaps the fords where cattle would once have crossed the river nearby. A Pictish-style snake also appears, its serpentine form reminiscent of the Don as it winds its way past Kemnay.

The north side of the stone features a carving of a salmon, an important Pictish symbol, similar to that seen on the Craw Stane at Rhynie. Recent research has suggested that the Picts avoided eating fish for cultural or spiritual reasons despite being able seafarers.[3]

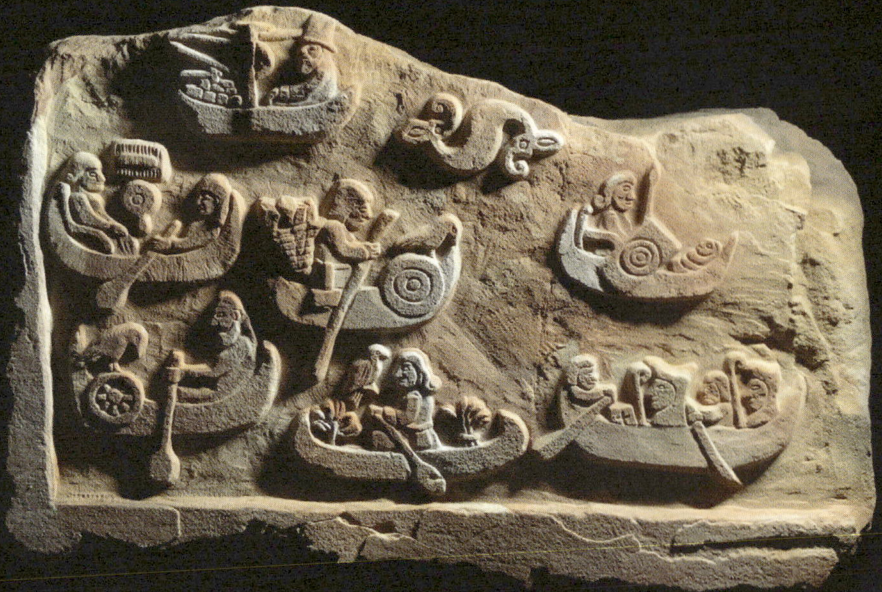

The Shakkin Briggie Steen

Positioned on the east bank of the river, at the top of the footpath that leads to the Shakkin Briggie, this stone features a series of boats competing in the annual raft race. Each boat represents one of the other Kemnay Steens. The stone is covered in swirling patterns left 320 million years ago when it was formed from the action of water.

The Cailleach can be seen carrying a basket of rocks and a giant hammer, both of which she used to shape the mountains and lochs. In her hand is a staff capable of freezing the ground as she takes her throne over winter. George Burnett of Kemnay and his parrot can be seen below with an oat sheaf onboard and a young sapling ready for planting.

Towards the back are Jock o' Bennachie and the Kemnay Fair Queen. At the front two monks and their attendants travel downstream after a visit to Fetternear, with the Warrior Mother from the Mither Tap Steen not far behind.

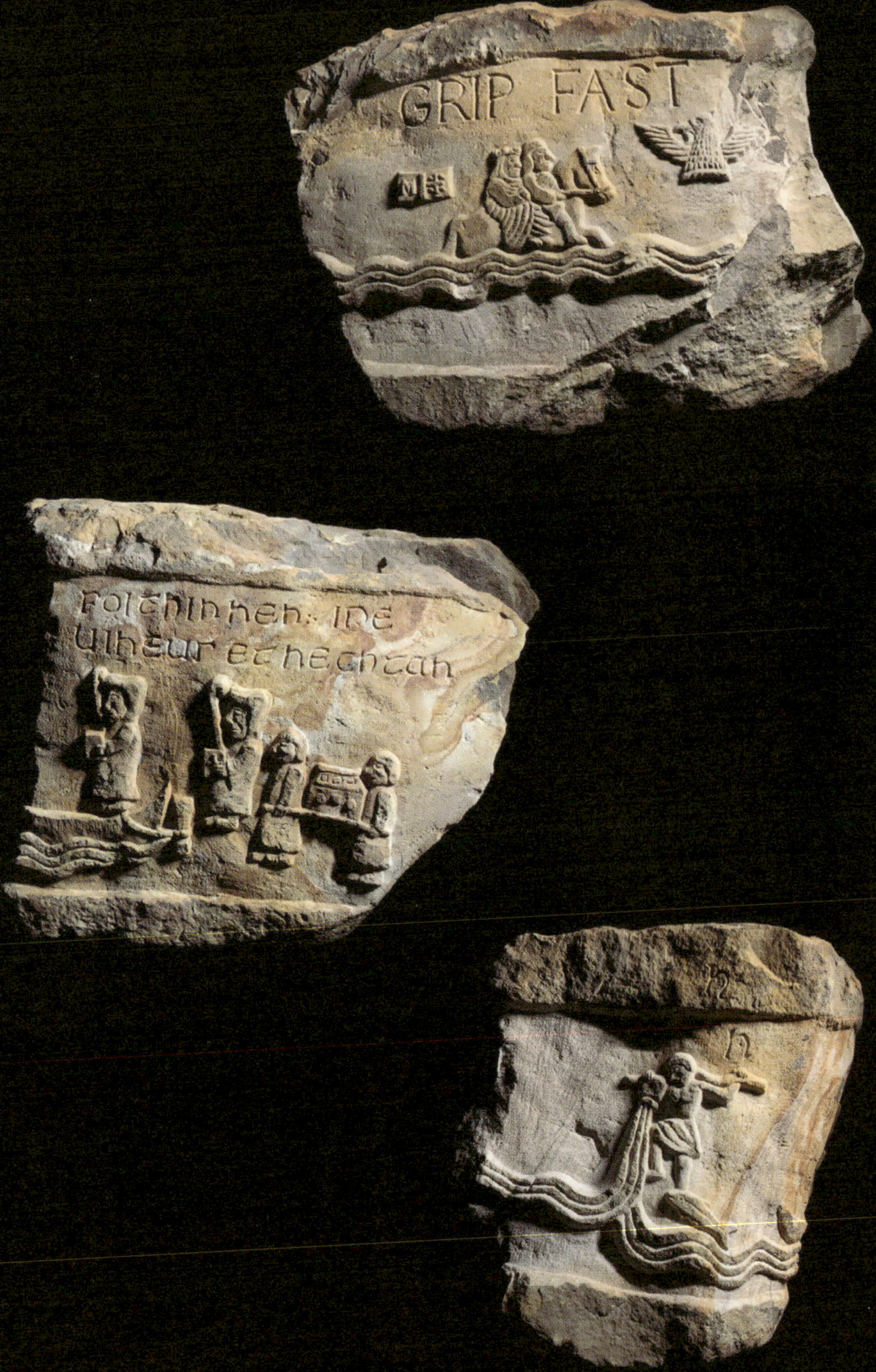
GRIP FAST

The Fetternear Steen

This stone lies in mature woodland within the Fetternear Estate. It can be found alongside a track near Bankhead Pool on the north bank of the river Don. One side of the stone shows two people on horseback fording a river. The figures reference the origins of the Leslies of Balquhain (of Fetternear).

In 1067, a nobleman named Bartolf came to Scotland from Hungary in the court of Princess Margaret. Margaret was later to become the Queen of Malcolm III and eventually St Margaret of Scotland. Malcolm III made Bartolf the first governor of Edinburgh Castle and gave him land in Fife, Angus and Aberdeenshire.

As the Queen's Chamberlain, it is said that Bartolf once helped Margaret cross a swollen river on horseback. During the crossing the horse stumbled and the Queen, fearing she would fall cried, "Gin the buckle bide?!" Bartolf answered, "Grip fast!" and they made it across. He was so alarmed by the incident that he had two more buckles added to his belt.

Bartolf built a castle at Lesselyn in the Garioch, which is the origin of the Leslie name. A belt with three buckles became the Leslie arms and 'Grip Fast' became the motto. A griffin on the right of the stone carving is similar to a griffin still visible in the coat of arms above the door of Fetternear House, along with the fading remnants of the 'Grip Fast' motto.

The other side of the stone features two monks and their attendants with a boat moored at Fetternear. A text above them reads, 'FOITHIRNER IRE UINEUS ET NECHTAN'. Some of the wording is similar to a text on the 9th century Drosten Stone from St Vigeans near Arbroath. 'Foithir ner' (Fetternear) can be translated as the slope of Ner which has been linked with an entry in the Irish chronicles mentioning the death of an Abbot Uineus of Ner in 623.[4] Another entry mentions the death in 679 of a St Nechtan or Nechtan Ner, potentially linked to an early monastic settlement nearby. The text therefore translates as, 'Fetternear in the time of Uineus and Nechtan'.

The monks' attendants carry a medieval reliquary which bears a resemblance to the early 8th century Monymusk Reliquary, one of the most important artefacts from the period, now at the National Museum of Scotland in Edinburgh. The Monymusk Reliquary was said to have once contained relics of St. Columba. For a time in the 19th century it was understood to be the 'Brecbennoch of St. Columba', a sacred battle ensign of the Scottish army, used for saintly assistance at the Battle of Bannockburn in 1314.

The carving on the end of the stone shows the source of the rivers which appear on the other carvings. Here they are shown being poured by a figure with a salmon at his feet, perhaps representative of the 'salmon of knowledge', believed to contain all the wisdom in the world. The figure may represent Nechtan or Nodens, who in Celtic mythology is often associated with wells and springs. Nechtan was a common name for Pictish kings. The figure also takes the form of the constellation Aquarius, the water carrier.

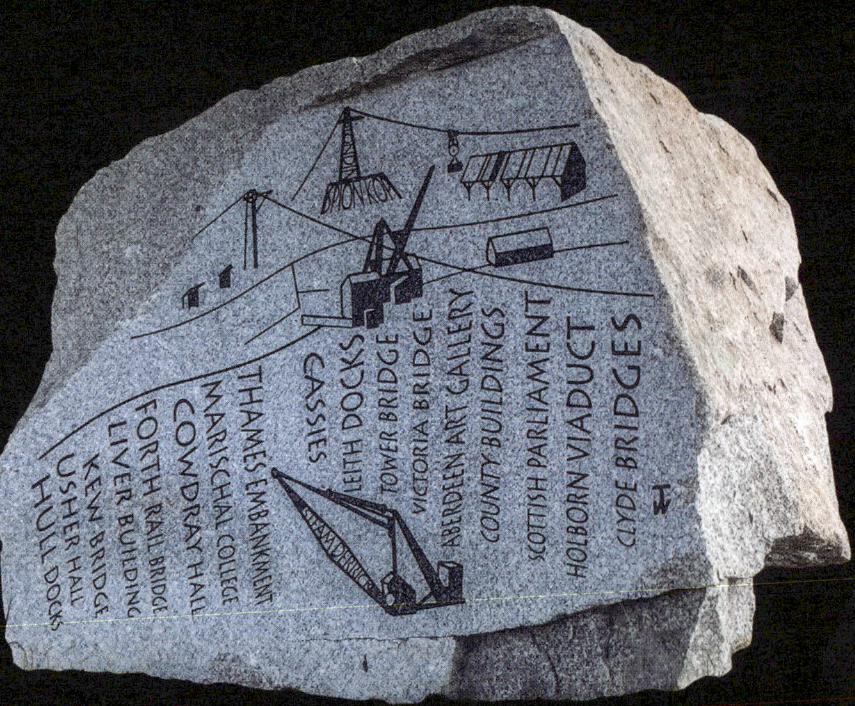
CLYDE BRIDGES
HOLBORN VIADUCT
SCOTTISH PARLIAMENT
COUNTY BUILDINGS
ABERDEEN ART GALLERY
VICTORIA BRIDGE
TOWER BRIDGE
LEITH DOCKS
CASSIES
THAMES EMBANKMENT
MARISCHAL COLLEGE
COWDRAY HALL
FORTH RAIL BRIDGE
LIVER BUILDING
KEW BRIDGE
USHER HALL
HULL DOCKS
STEAM DERRICK

The Quarry Steen

This two-tonne block of granite sits alongside a footpath in Dalmadilly adjacent to the junction with Aquithie Road. It was quarried just 200m away at Kemnay Quarry and a line of drill holes from the quarrying process are still visible on one side. The design has been sandblasted into the granite with a black infill then added. The granite itself would have been formed over 400 million years ago and is close-grained and extremely hard.

The granite industry in Kemnay was revolutionised by the arrival of John Fyfe in 1858, which led to massive changes in the village. Although granite had been quarried in Kemnay on a small scale, it was only with the arrival of the railway that the industry really flourished. In 1858, while the railway was being built, John Fyfe took a lease of the Paradise Hill quarry. It was ideally placed with the railway once running exactly where this stone stands today.

The design on the stone shows a steam derrick for moving blocks of stone at the quarry floor. This major technical advancement was developed through John Fyfe's conversations with Andrew Barclay, a young engineer in Kilmarnock. The Scottish steam derrick allowed Fyfe to quarry downwards for better stone rather than just into the hill – a development that revolutionised quarrying worldwide. The main quarry would eventually reach a depth of 122m.

A few years later John Fyfe saw a postman pass a bag of mail across the Dee at Abergeldie by means of an endless rope. This gave him the idea for the steam powered 'Blondin' – a travelling carriage suspended from an endless cable that could be lowered to retrieve stone from the quarry floor. Stones could then be transferred directly into the mason's shed (shown on the right of the stone) through special roof openings. Named after Charles Blondin, a French tightrope walker, Fyfe's invention became standard equipment in quarries internationally, with Kemnay's Blondin able to lift blocks weighing 100 tonnes.

An artificial raised platform was built to house one of the steel lattice towers for the Blondin. This became known as 'Spion Kop' after a hill of the same name in a battle of the Boer War. The design on the stone also shows a crane at the pit edge from where quarrymen would be lowered in hutches and two huts known as 'scathies' where road setts or 'cassies' were made.

The walls of the quarry list a small selection of the various projects where Kemnay granite has been used.

References

1. Downie, D.A. (2009) George Burnett landscape designer, Improvements on Kemnay Estate during the 18th Century, Kemnay: Time Pieces.
2. National Library of Scotland, Moving Image Archive, Kemnay Fair 1976, Available at: https://movingimage.nls.uk/film/8786 (Accessed: 18th November 2020).
3. Curtis-Summers, S., Pearson, J.A. and Lamb, A.L. (2020) 'From Picts to Parish: Stable isotope evidence of dietary change at medieval Portmahomack, Scotland,', Journal of Archaeological Science: Reports , Volume 31(102303)
4. Clancy, T.O. (2008) 'Deer and the early church in North-Eastern Scotland', in Forsyth, K. (ed.) Studies on the book of Deer. Dublin: Four Courts Press, pp. 363-97.

Further Reading

Ango, A.C. and Downie, D.A. (1996) John Fyfe, One hundred and fifty years 1846-1996, Kemnay: Time Pieces.

Archibald, M. (1996) Scottish animal and bird folklore, Edinburgh: Saint Andrew Press.

Downie, D.A. (2000) From the Wilderness to Paradise, Developments in agriculture on Kemnay Estate from the Mid 18th Century to the Mid 19th Century, Kemnay: Time Pieces.

Downie, D.A. (2008) The Kirktown of Kemnay: being a short description of the changes in the area over the last two hundred years, Kemnay: Time Pieces.

Jones, D. (2014) A wee guide to the Picts, 8th edn., Musselburgh: Goblinshead.

McConnochie, A.I. (1897) Bennachie, 2nd edn., Aberdeen: Lewis Smith & Son.

Milne, J. (1947) 'Twixt Ury and Don and round about, Inverurie: Dufton Scott & Son.

Noble, G. and Evans, N. (2019) The King in the North, The Pictish Realms of Fortriu and Ce, Edinburgh: Birlinn.

Royal Commission on the Ancient and Historical Monuments of Scotland (2008) In the shadow of Bennachie, 2nd edn., Edinburgh: RCAHMS.

Shepherd, C. (Ed.) (2019) Bennachie and the Garioch: Society and ecology in the history of North East Scotland: The Bailies of Bennachie.

Whiteley, A.W.M. (Ed.) (1976) The book of Bennachie: The Bailies of Bennachie.

Whiteley, A.W.M. (Ed.) (1983) Bennachie again: The Bailies of Bennachie.

Thanks

Thanks to: Lorna Forsyth, Sarah Franklin, Susie Hunt, Naida Sneddon, Jenny Spratt, Craig Thomson, Sue Wainman, Sheila Waterhouse.

Additional thanks to: Gillian Adam, Murdo Adam, Kemnay Academy, George Andrew, Lorna Bell, Bailies of Bennachie, Neale Bisset, Breedon, Alex Burnett, Vhari Cairns, Richard Collinson, Sarah Daly, Duncan Downie, David Fyffe, Adam Gandy, Fyfe Glenrock, Kemnay Guides, Hilda Hart, Andy Henderson, Kemnay Kestrels, Rob Mackay, Midge Manson, Griselda McGregor, Positive Steps Kemnay, Studio Pavilion, Peter Robinson, Roderick Scott, Kemnay Scouts, Allan Stronach, Alison Sutherland, Sue Taylor, Billy Teasdale.

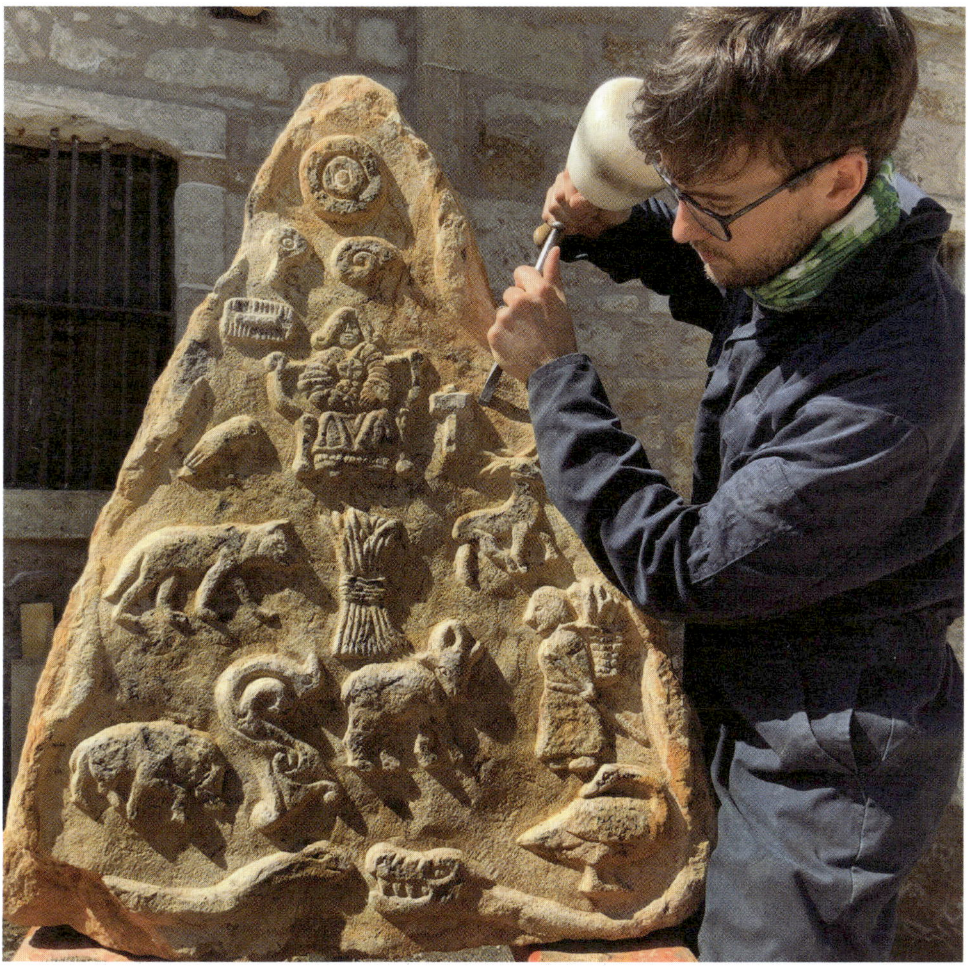

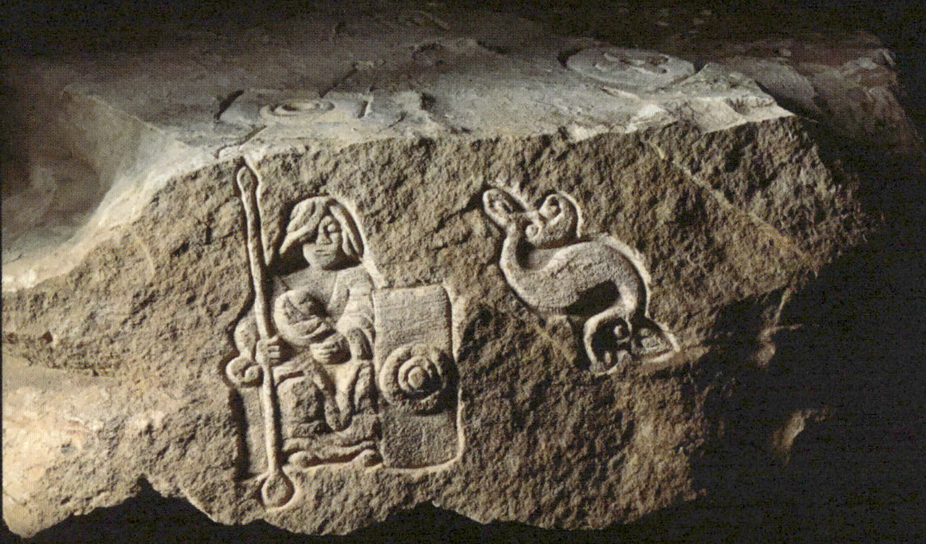